FACET BOOKS

SOCIAL ETHICS SERIES

FACET **fb** BOOKS

SOCIAL ETHICS SERIES—15

Franklin Sherman, General Editor

Christian Decision
in the
Nuclear Age

by T. R. MILFORD

FORTRESS PRESS   PHILADELPHIA

Reprinted, with revisions, by arrangement with
the British Council of Churches, London

Library of Congress Catalog Card Number 67-13058

3679K66   Printed in U.S.A.   1-3038

Introduction

THIS essay by Canon T. R. Milford is valuable both as an analysis of Christian decision-making in general, and as a commentary on the particular problem of war and peace as it confronts mankind at the present time.

What are the factors that should enter into decisions made by Christians on controversial social questions? What is the role of biblical teaching, of precedents in church history, of intuitive grasp of the situation? Are Christians always called to be dissenters, or can they in good conscience enter into the structures of power and speak on behalf of "the many" as well as "the few"? These are some of the questions dealt with by Milford in his first and more general chapters.

Then, after a transitional chapter on the church's past attitudes toward war, the author turns to a discussion of the present international situation, as it has developed through one crisis after another since 1914. He is critical of the part played by the churches in Britain and America in fostering pacifist sentiment, especially during the 1930's; and yet he is equally vigorous in criticizing the tendency to identify God's cause with the cause of the West (or of "democracy" or "the free world"). The Christian pathway is seen to lie neither in an uncritical acceptance of the regnant ideology nor in an opting out of social responsibility, but rather in a middle way, which can so easily be labeled and dismissed as "compromise." The final chapters explore what this middle way might mean for the difficult problems of maintaining peace and moving toward new structures of world order in this nuclear age.

The author, Theodore Richard Milford, has had a distinguished career in the Church of England. After serving for nearly a decade as vicar of the University Church of St. Mary the Virgin in Oxford, he now holds the position of Master of the Temple, i.e., chaplain to two of the Inns of Court, London's historic law schools. He served also as chairman of the Oxford Committee for Famine Relief, one of Britain's leading agencies for overseas aid and development. From 1947 to 1958 he was chancellor of Lincoln Cathedral. A volume of Canon Milford's sermons has been published under the title *Foolishness to the Greeks* (London: SCM Press, 1953; and Greenwich, Conn.: Seabury Press, 1954).

The present essay resulted from discussions during the period 1957 to 1961 by a working party appointed by the British Council of Churches to discuss "Moral Aspects of Disarmament." Among the other members of the group were Robert C. Mackie (chairman), Sir Anthony Buzzard, Sir Kenneth Grubb, Alan R. Booth, Daniel T. Jenkins, and Kenneth Johnstone. A statement entitled *Christians and Atomic War* was produced by the group and published by the British Council of Churches in 1959. Further discussions then led to the writing of the present pamphlet, for which Canon Milford served as author, although drafts were discussed by the whole group. It was first published by the British Council of Churches in 1961 under the title *The Valley of Decision: The Christian Dilemma in the Nuclear Age.* For this Facet Books edition, the text has been revised by the author in the light of subsequent developments and in order to address the argument more specifically to an American audience.

FRANKLIN SHERMAN

Lutheran School of Theology at Chicago
October, 1966

Contents

1

THE MEANING OF DECISION

A decision takes place when someone's mind is brought to bear on a particular situation. The result may be an overt act, which may set in train a whole series of other acts not requiring fresh decisions. I may decide to go by a certain train; getting up, catching the bus, booking my ticket, and going on board follow on from that. Other people's actions may follow too. I decide to order beer; the barman doesn't have to decide to give me beer. But a decision may not issue in an overt act. It may be the registering of an attitude. If this has been a real decision the appropriate overt acts will be triggered off by circumstances without any fresh decision at all. The barman decided to take that job; serving beer to customers when they order it follows of its own accord.

Decisions are important even if they do not lead to any immediate overt act; for the serious and responsible registering of an attitude may have far reaching results and take effect when we have no time to think.

Decisions are often taken jointly, leading to overt action in the case of the Cabinet and other committees holding executive power. But they may also register a common attitude, like a resolution at a public meeting. These can also be important if those who pass the resolution are sincerely convinced.

Many attitudes are purely habitual, unconsidered, or due to prejudice. According to the psychologists we are often unaware of the real reason for our attitudes. Deep influences of high emotional voltage deflect and distort our vision. A rational decision will allow for this, and try to discount it. But since no one can be entirely rational, least of all when his own interests are involved, it is necessary also to allow for the possibility of mistake. One way of combat-

1

ing prejudice is really to listen to someone who is sincerely convinced on the other side. This may make decision harder, but when it is made, it is better based. It is also a good thing when possible to take decisions in periods of comparative calm, so that they are ready when a crisis comes.

Prejudice is harder to combat when it is backed up by the crowd. Class, nation, and race are particularly powerful, and give the impression that what "we" think must be right. The remedy is to see ourselves as others see us, and that means listening and using imagination. And *that* means love.

Decisions are made by statesmen without consulting us, often without our knowledge. They are in fact largely determined by attitudes taken long before by many people, and which the statesmen consciously or unconsciously share. Public opinion is a real force, and we can help to form it, not only on the rare occasions when we vote. It is because *we* want TV sets and tobacco and income tax kept down that *they* do not decide to give more to underdeveloped countries. It is because everybody is scared that no one can disarm.

CHRISTIAN DECISION

The attitudes and decisions of Christians may be as irrational and prejudiced as anyone's, or even more so; for inherited prejudice and the influence of the group (church, denomination, or party) may be given divine sanction and become immune to criticism. But it need not be so. Christian decision in the proper sense occurs when the holy will of God is brought to bear on a particular situation; and the individual Christian, by himself or acting with others, can be and should be the agent through which this happens.

The conditions on the human side seem to be something like this. The Christian in worship, Bible reading, and prayer, attends to and assents to the holy will of God and his purpose for the world and for himself. This leads to repentance, in which he admits and wants to discount his own prejudice, selfish desires, and fears. It leads to faith renewed, whereby he offers to God his own imperfect wisdom, his own distorted vision, and his own uncertain will, to make what use God can of them. As far as he is able, he draws upon the accumulated wisdom of the church, and calls to his aid the example of the saints, which help him to discount the immediate pressure of his environment. There are rules to help him, which he will not go against without grave cause. And equally he will be in living union with his contemporary world; in the case of his immediate neighbors, by having really met them and cared about them. In political decisions he will also have to have made himself acquainted with the relevant facts, by reading or in other ways. In all this there is much that cannot be improvised; a responsible Christian cannot be grown overnight. For in principle all that he has done, all that he has received, all that he knows, all that he is, is brought to bear at the point of decision. In the end it is *his* decision, and no one but he could have made it. That is what he is there for.

THE GUIDANCE OF THE HOLY SPIRIT

This is the kind of way in which the Holy Spirit guides—not by dictating ready-made answers. In Isaiah 11 the necessary gifts are promised to the Messiah for his peculiar work of establishing God's kingdom; and they are described in three pairs, where each of the pair corrects and supplements the other. The spirit of wisdom and understanding: for wisdom is the ability to see all round the question, and understanding the ability to see the precise point at issue. The spirit of counsel and might: for counsel is the ability to know what ought to be done, and might is the power to see it through. Knowledge and the fear of the Lord: for knowledge is what the theologian has, and the fear of the Lord is religious devotion. A knowledge of theology is useless by itself, and devotion is positively dangerous if the idea of God which it inspires is false.

It is our belief that when we put our intelligence and will and affections to the job of making and carrying through decisions in a Christian way, and in fellowship with one another, we can become the agents of a good and intelligent will greater than our own, greater than that of those who agree with us, than that of the actual church or any nation, or of mankind as it actually exists. We have seen this Spirit in Christ, we can trace its working in the Bible and in the history of the church, and we believe that it is still at work today.

We concentrate our attention on the Bible and church history because there are the roots from which Christians and their decisions grow. But we must never forget that the same God who was working in this very peculiar fashion on Israel and carrying on in the church was maintaining the fabric of the world and all the other nations. Egypt was not *only* there to be escaped from. The 120,000 Assyrian children in Nineveh were dear to God and presumably to their mothers too. Babylonian astronomers were inventing the duodecimal system; their engineers were irrigating the Mesopotamian plain. Greeks were meditating on the eternal laws of right and wrong and human destiny; Indians were seeking the peace which passes understanding; Chinese were laying down the principles of civilized life; nameless and numberless people who have no history, in Africa and the Americas, were managing to survive in the primeval forest and passing on their wisdom in myth and ritual.

Consequently, Christians are not the only people who matter. Our opinion, even if we could agree, does not necessarily represent the total will or the whole wisdom of God, nor do we control the course of history. Our thesis is that at this crucial point in time, when all the peoples who have developed hitherto in partial isolation are being inexorably pressed together, we have (not of our own deserving, but by God's grace) a privileged access to the central mystery, a saving word which can only be spoken at the cost of a resolute involvement in the world's affairs and an imaginative caring which goes much deeper, and in the result is more productive, than agreement on a policy which we have no power to enforce. Twenty years after, nobody cares or wants to know whether you were a pacifist or not. Whether you loved or hated, whether you hardened your heart or stayed humble: that is what mattered then and that is what matters still.

The formula of the Many and the Few is derived from an experience of constantly being forced to think again when a question had seemed closed; from a reading of history; from an experience of living in India; from trying constantly to relate the biblical story with the facts as otherwise known, and to believe that the God of nature and the God of grace are one and the same. It is dialectical in one sense of that slippery word. It has proved to be a suggestive clue in interpreting the Bible story (where the "saving remnant" embodies one-half of the antithesis) as well as church history and the working of democracy. It picked up its watchword from the mouth of Jonathan, "Nothing can hinder the Lord from saving by many or by few" (I Sam. 14:6), without implying that Jonathan would have agreed with it, for presumably he did not know that the Lord had brought up those Philistines from Caphtor.

We can as Christians only speak on these subjects at all in a spirit of penitence for the many fearful blots in the record of the church, for the crimes and stupidities committed in the name of Christ, and for the blindness, stupidity, and selfishness which still beset us. In the light of our record and the record of the nations of Christendom it is small matter for wonder if the world will not hear. But true penitence is a change of mind and heart, which is not only sorry for the past, but really wants to do better. And so our penitence must include not only acknowledging our ancestors' errors (which is easy), not only admitting in a general way that we are not much better (which is only decent), but a continual re-examination in the light of our Lord's known will of our own established conclusions and familiar habits, with the promise in advance that where we are wrong we are willing to be changed. This is hard indeed, but we can help one another to it if we speak—and listen—in love.

2

CHRISTIAN DECISION AND THE BIBLE

THE Bible can be used in many ways, and some of them are dangerous. It has often been used as a source book for texts chosen to prove some conviction which the user had already. In the wars of religion, Catholics and Protestants appealed to the same book, and sometimes to the very same texts, to support their own positions, and claimed divine authority for their views rather than give way. "Thou shalt not suffer a witch to live" justified the burning of many crazed old women, and the divine command that Israel should exterminate its enemies made it seem right for Christians to do the same. Even in the New Testament support could be found for the claims of the pope and for the duty of resistance to the pope, for obedience to the "powers that be" and for rebellion against them, for pacifism and the just war, for a world-denying ethic and the acceptance and use of wealth and all good things.

More plausible today is to read the Bible as a history book and to draw "lessons" from it which can be applied in our own time. Isaiah told Ahaz and Hezekiah that they should not trust in alliances; therefore we should not make alliances. Nehemiah's men built with one hand and kept a spear ready in the other. Therefore we should "negotiate from strength." It is true that there are lessons to be learned from the Bible which are true for all time, for we do see God working there, the same God who is working now; but they are not to be discovered so simply. One reason is that the history of Israel–Christ –church, which is the main subject of the Bible, is unique, and in seeking there for precedents it is only too easy to suppose that "we" (Britain or the West, or in the case of other people, some other "we") are in the position of Israel, and our enemies are represented by the

Amalekites, Babylonians, and the rest. (So Kruger in the South African War applied the words of Psalm 83, "They have said, Come and let us root them out, that they be no more a people," to Britain, and turned the whole Psalm into a prayer against us; and there are many other instances.) The Old Testament has to pass through the crucifixion and resurrection before it can be used by Christians. Nor can we directly apply precedents from Israel's history to the church in which it is continued, and identify the enemies of Israel with the enemies of the church. Even if we could, we have been commanded to love them, which Israel never did.

Moreover, though the good will of God is constant, the situation in which it has to be embodied is never the same; and if there is one clear "lesson" which does emerge from the Bible, it is that God was always taking people by surprise, especially when they were most convinced that he was going to repeat himself. There are two outstanding instances. One is this. Jerusalem had been saved from the Assyrians by the word of Isaiah in Hezekiah's reign. Therefore when the Babylonians came 120 years after, Zedekiah thought the same thing would happen again, and it was Jeremiah's unpleasant duty to say: on the contrary; this time your only chance is to surrender. The second main instance is the crucial one. The Maccabees had led a successful revolt against the Greeks, and therefore 200 years later the Zealots thought God would save them if they rebelled against the Romans. He failed to do so, and the terrible siege and fall of Jerusalem was the result. Actually God *had* intervened to save his people, but in such a surprising way that Jerusalem did not recognize the day of her visitation, and demanded the crucifixion of her Lord.

And yet, if they had known, the clues were there. The God who saved before was still the God who saves. The God who had promised to establish his kingdom would surely establish it. The God who had summoned his people to be holy still called them to be holy. He who had promised to dwell among them was preparing to do so in truth. But only Jesus could see through the various and partial fulfillments of the promises to the one act which should make them all come true.

How We Read the Bible

For our purpose here we shall take as our central clue the emergence of the People of God called out of the nations of the world to be "holy," that is, a dedicated people, living for purposes not of their own choosing, purposes not confined to life in this world, but to be worked out in this world as the place of their present obedience. This people have their place in this world, and serious dealings with their neighbors in this world, but the ultimate reference points by which they are directed and judged are "out of this world"; and that is what makes their obedience and disobedience so important. The story tells how they are progressively being trained to see what this means—and they do not like it!

But we shall also look for clues to discover how at each point the people concerned made their decisions, and did or did not fulfill the will of God. That is, we shall look on each incident not only as a link in the chain, but also as a place where we can, as it were, hear God speaking, or see him at work. These come to the same thing, for when God speaks things happen.

These somewhat enigmatic remarks are now to be illustrated by a few selected instances. Within our limits they can only be briefly indicated. They will only come alive in the actual reading of the Bible itself, marking, learning, *and* inwardly digesting it.

Moses and the Exodus

"The Lord . . . has triumphed gloriously; the horse and his rider he has thrown into the sea." The echoes of that triumph are heard throughout the Old Testament and the New, as the first great example of the action of the God who saves. What exactly happened in terms of physical events such as could have been recorded by the camera, we shall presumably never know. But in view of what followed we must see there the birth of the Holy People. Quite probably not all the tribes who afterwards joined together to form Israel were in Egypt at all. For some of them the deliverance from Sisera may have been the formative experience. However this may be, as they grew together and celebrated together in psalms and dances with trumpets and cymbals, they identified the hand of the same Lord in both great victories, and understood them in the same way, as a call to belong henceforth to him alone. They attributed their conquests and colonization of Palestine, which began under the first Joshua, to the same Lord, and thanked him for the ready-made cities and fertile fields which he gave into their possession.

If Moses had not existed it would have been necessary to invent him; for surely there was some great man there who could seize the opportunity and make it what it in fact became, the beginning of a new and unique thing injected into the general stream of the world's history—what we have called the Holy People. Called to be holy, that is to belong to God who had saved and saves; bound by a loyalty which on their part called for the observance of a moral standard which was higher than that of their neighbors and continually rising; held together by a faith in their own God, which by its own intrinsic logic would end up by being faith in the one and only God of all the world. They were called for a purpose which reached far beyond themselves, for if their faith was true it was the faith which all the nations must in the end be brought to recognize.

"This," said Moses and all the prophets (or, if you prefer a Moses-shaped gap to Moses, just all the prophets) "is the thing which was beginning at the Exodus, and the end we can't see yet." *We* can't see the end yet either, but we are further down the line, and in the light of what has happened since, we have still stronger grounds than they had for believing that Moses and the prophets were right. And if we asked them how they knew, they could point in the first place to their escape and their arrival in due course at their new home. But it was not just a rational inference from events, a shrewd reading of the signs of the times. The faith in God came first, before the wonders that confirmed it. It was a response to a total uncompromising demand, "You shall have no other gods before me"; and it took the form of a total committal, now a venturing into the midst of the waters of the Red Sea or the Jordan, now a venturing of lives in battle, a repudiation of graven images or the observance of a dietary rule. It was a demand to come out from among the nations and be different. On their side it was that; and they trusted that God would observe his part by seeing them through. This was "the Covenant."

They were seen through. They did arrive. They did take over the cities. Saul set up a kingdom, which made them feel respectable, but he fell foul of Samuel. David was appointed in his place. Jerusalem was conquered and became the citadel of the Lord's anointed. Solomon built a temple for the Lord to settle down in, and that, it might seem, was that. The Holy People had arrived.

In fact they had only reached an inn, a temporary camping place which could not last. Not by such methods could the abiding city of lasting peace be founded, on war and massacre and intrigue. Nor could it be maintained by Solomon's methods, cunning alliances, multiple diplomatic marriages, booming trade, high taxation, and royal display. Solomon's son was just silly and it all broke up. Judah split from Israel, idolatry returned, and a sickening period followed, of futile wars and short-lived truces. The great powers after a temporary period of weakness were stirring again, and the squabbling infants, Judah, Israel, and Syria, found themselves in no man's land.

Yet it is in this tragic period that the great prophets begin to see further what it means to believe in the God who saves, and the conditions of obedience. The other nations are brought into the picture, in the first place as the indispensable background for God's dealings with Israel. Amos asserts that the Lord brought up the Philistines from Caphtor and the Syrians from Kir, no less than the Israelites out of Egypt. He declares God's judgments on Moab and the rest for breaking the moral law, but this is merely preliminary to the main point, which is God's judgment on Israel. Assyria, Babylon, Egypt, and Persia appear to exist almost entirely in order that God may use them to do things to Israel and Judah. This limitation of the prophets' view makes it impossible to learn anything from them about the purpose of God in creating India and China and the South Sea islands, but they were committed to a belief which would eventually bring that question too above the horizon.

They said also, with a devastating emphasis which sometimes swept everything else aside, that the only conditions for being acceptable to God are the practice of justice and the observance of the moral law. They even appear to regard worship as irrelevant. "Who requires of you this trampling of my courts? . . . I cannot endure iniquity and solemn assembly." This is what it now meant to be holy to the Lord, to obey his righteous will. It seemed to follow that if they observed his law, God must keep his part of the covenant by rewarding them with long life and happiness, which includes good harvests, victory in war, and peace to enjoy these things. Deuteronomy may be said to summarize this view, which is also expressed at great length by Job's comforters. It seemed to be confirmed when Jerusalem was saved in Hezekiah's reign. Questions might be raised when Manasseh, who revived idolatry and ruled so badly, reigned for fifty-five years and was buried with his fathers. They were raised acutely when his grandson Josiah carried out a reformation inspired by Deuteronomy, and was promised by Huldah the prophetess that he should be gathered to his grave in peace, and should not see the evil which the Lord would bring upon Israel. In fact, however, he crossed Pharaoh Necho and was executed. Not long after, Jerusalem was taken by the Babylonians as Jeremiah foretold, and the kingdom came to an end forever.

Once more the prophets' message had turned out to be too simple. "I have been young, and now am old; yet I have not seen the righteous forsaken or his children begging bread." So said the psalmist, and all one can say is that he was either remarkably fortunate, or lacked imagination.

If at this point we pause, and try to listen in on the prophets as they seek to know the will of God, we have their own words to go on. Firstly we must realize that each of them started at a point where much had already happened, and the Lord was already the accepted God of Israel. Their question is not, "Does God exist?" nor yet, "How many gods are there?" but, "What is the Lord (that is, the God of Abraham, Isaac, Jacob and Moses and David) saying to me now?" Amos in the desert looking after his sheep and sycamore trees got a sudden conviction that he must go and protest against the corruption of city life and city worship. With that conviction he looked at the international situation and saw with some accuracy from which direction the expected doom was going to come. Isaiah as a young man suddenly saw the real meaning of worship as offered in the temple, and saw what Israel and himself must look like from the point of view of the holy God. Repentant and painfully purged he could volunteer for service, and was given a severe and terrible message to deliver, which followed logically from what he had seen the "holy" to mean, in conjunction with what he knew his people to be like. He was not afraid to interfere in politics; he attempted with some success to direct the foreign policy of his kings, and knowing God as he did and the needs of his ill-led people, he promised the coming into David's line of a ruler who should do indeed what David had failed to do, and what he himself could only partly do, and make the kingdom of God on earth a reality. But when and how this would be, he could not know. In Jeremiah's time things were much worse, and still believing in the goodwill of the holy God, he shrank from proclaiming the obvious conclusion. But he had to proclaim it, protesting often against its seeming hardness. Precluded from seeing any hopeful future in political terms he promised and foretold an inward revolution, and a race of converted men with God's law written in their hearts.

11

A vision of God, inherited, but apprehended at first hand, and therefore going further than the inherited faith, and a willing or reluctant recognition of the facts, both moral and political: where these two meet the Lord is heard to speak, and the prophet has no choice but to proclaim what he has heard.

THE EFFECT OF THE EXILE

The disaster of the exile fell on all alike, whether they had tried to obey the demands of the Lord or not, but it was felt most severely by those who loved Jerusalem and the worship of the temple and longed to return to it. Somewhere at this point the prophet whom we know as the second Isaiah saw deeper into the cost of obedience and the meaning of suffering. He saw that the faithful servant of the Lord may have to suffer for the faults of others and that by his suffering the many can be saved. "Yet we esteemed him stricken, smitten by God, and afflicted. . . and the Lord has laid on him the iniquity of us all." Whom had he in mind? The famous fifty-third chapter of Isaiah has been held to refer to the whole people of Israel, or to a small faithful nucleus, or to one individual such as Jeremiah himself. There are phrases in it which make each of these views seem plausible. But is it necessary to decide? Had the prophet himself this in mind, that somehow it must work out? If Israel could take its sufferings that way it would itself be raised from the dead and lead the nations into the way of peace. If not Israel then some in Israel might do it, for there had already been indications in the first Isaiah that the few might suffer for the many.

The same prophet foretold a splendid restoration for Jerusalem and a period of just rule, peace, and prosperity which should manifest to all the nations the righteousness of the Lord and vindicate his people. In fact the historical fulfillment was disappointing. The kingdom was not restored, corruption again set in, and the other nations did not see the glory of God in what had happened.

Once again, in the second century before Christ, the faith was in deadly peril. The desperate revolt of the Maccabees was for a time successful, but this also turned out to be only temporary, and finally the weight of Rome came down over the whole area and brought a kind of peace.

All these disappointments were compensated for in what we call the apocalyptic books by more and more fantastic expectations of a divine irruption which, in the end, lost all touch with reality.

"These things were written down for our instruction," and we may perhaps summarize the lessons to be learned from the Old Testament in a few short sentences:

1. There is a continuing divine purpose in history. It is particularly clear in that of Israel and we must believe that it includes other streams as well.

2. There is a recurring pattern by which a start is made with one or a few, followed by expansion, perhaps by corruption, and a fresh start with one or a few. The pattern is not one of steady progress, but more like death and resurrection. In detail it is always new and surprising.

3. The thing which is saved by many or by few is connected, but not identified, with the actual people of Israel and "it" may be saved by what for Israel is a disaster.

4. The reward of righteousness is a blessing, but this does not necessarily feel like a blessing. It may consist in the power to be faithful even through disaster and death.

5. The will of God is always particular and is discovered at the growing points where a traditional faith is brought to bear on circumstances.

6. The prophets do not control the great nations but, believing that God does, they prepare their own people so that what the nations do will work out for good through them.

NEW TESTAMENT

We find the same general pattern in the New Testament, only here the faithful remnant is reduced to one, who in his death does what Israel could not do for itself, and dies for the sake of the world. We are allowed at certain points, e.g., the temptations in the wilderness and in Gethsemane, to overhear Jesus as he discovers God's will. On the one hand he made his own the faith which demanded that God should vindicate His people and bring to earth in reality what had only been hinted at in David's kingdom, Solomon's temple, and the people who lived by observing the law. On the other hand we find him dealing in a completely realistic way with the actual situation. The Holy People had reached a crisis, the crisis of holiness itself. They had been taught by grim experience the dangers of compromise, so that the meticulous observance of the law had become the fence which separated them from the heathen. But this very thing prevented them from loving or forgiving the Romans who ruled them, the Greeks who laughed at them, and most of all the "publicans and sinners" among themselves who compromised and would not keep the rules. Thus as we read the Gospels we see how the controversies developed on these very points. Christ began at the very center, with his own people. "Go rather to the lost sheep of the house of Israel." And so he mixed with the publicans and sinners, and invited them into his company just as they were, offering free forgiveness without limit, and at the same time demanded self-giving without limit from those who would follow him. It was possible to set oneself to obey the law, and the best of the Pharisees very nearly did it. But his line was too dangerous, and so he had to die. He could no doubt have escaped and gone on a preaching tour to the more liberal of the Dispersion, and from there to the Gentiles. But that was to be Paul's job. His own was to bring about the death and remaking of the few. The effort to put themselves in the right made his people hand him over to Pilate; the few who loved him let him down. And so the Old Testament bargain ("Obey the rules and God will bless you") broke down forever in the shameful, naked death of the perfect Israelite. And only those who loved him were reborn when they discovered that he lived and forgave and loved them still.

The cross is the supreme instance, suggested even in its shape, of the meeting at one point of the eternal purpose of God (read out of the Scriptures by the incomparable insight of Jesus) and the exact demands of the contemporary situation. Only God is completely consistent and radically opportunist, with an accuracy which general principles and statistical applications can never attain to.

Even the best laws make hard cases. God's own hard case, when he had dealt with it, made all the heavens ring with astonished praise.

The Many and the Few

Down to this point (roughly to the end of the New Testament) the process has been mainly one of concentration. The "many"—the other nations, Greece, and the Roman Empire—are in the background providing conditions of stability and opportunities for communication. Orthodox Israel is doing its best, but a best not good enough. These are the conditions, the necessary conditions, in which the creative spark can create the nucleus of the new life.

The example of Jesus and the ethics of the Sermon on the Mount define the calling of the creative minority, embodying the one thing needful, pointing the more perfect way. "Do not resist one who is evil. . . . Love your enemies and pray for those who persecute you. . . . Do not lay up for yourselves treasures on earth, where moth and rust consume. . . . Sell what you have, and give to the poor, and you will have treasure in heaven; and come, follow me. . . . If any one comes to me and does not hate his own father and mother and wife and children and brothers and sisters, yes, and even his own life, he cannot be my disciple. . . . If any one would sue you and take your coat, let him have your cloak as well. . . . Give to him who begs from you, and do not refuse him who would borrow from you."

It is important to take all these and similar sayings together, and not, as has often been done, to separate the pacifist ones from those dealing with property and going to law.

Indifference to the general ordering of society could hardly go further. Nor can this attitude be simply written off as a result of the expectation of the imminent end of the world. To "live each day as if thy last," to make no provision for the future—this is a way of living which does not depend on any supposed knowledge about "that day or that hour" when the end will come. It is the reflection of a faith in God so direct and immediate that dates and future prospects do not count. The only duty to this world which remains is the duty of witness, of which the characteristic method is by suffering. The only purpose served by the world is to be mission-fodder, and the various nations are judged by their reactions to Christ in his disciples. (This is a quite legitimate interpretation, perhaps the original intention, of the parable of the sheep and goats, which is usually taken to sanction works of mercy in general.)

If this were the whole story, the Pharisees would have been right in essentials, and the church ought to have been something like the Qumran community. Its subsequent history would be mainly a decline from its true destiny, and the conversion of the Empire in the fourth century the great disaster from which it has never recovered.

But there is another side to it. The new kind of holiness started, as we have seen, by taking risks and losing itself. The Lord did not protect himself from contamination by the world. He saw reflections of the goodness of God in ordinary human nature, not only in sanctified human nature, and in inanimate nature as well. He recognized, and told his disciples to recognize, the rights of Caesar in his own realm; he told Pilate that he would have no power if it were not given him "from above." St. Paul made use of his Roman citizenship to save himself a flogging, got a guard of Roman soldiers to avoid assassination, and as a prisoner lived in his own hired house and kept up correspondence with his friends a great deal more comfortably than if he had had no private means or influential friends. In his view the "powers that be" are ordained by God, the ruler "does not bear the sword in vain; he is the servant of God to execute his wrath on the wrongdoer." In I Peter the Christians are instructed to honor the emperor (though he was a pagan); and the closing vision of Revelation, where the nations walk by the light of the holy city and the kings of the earth bring the glory and honor of the nations into it, shows that they and their history are not completely written off as irrelevant.

If this is so, the disciples "sent out" into the world have a more dangerous mission. They have to remain "in the world." They have to come to terms with its thought—as then with Greek philosophy, so now with science. They have to adapt themselves to its technical advances, and as opportunity offers they have to accept responsibility in politics, including international affairs. A cup of cold water may expand into a whole enterprise of famine relief; oil and wine for dressing the wounds of a stranger imply medical missions and support for the World Health Organization. But the World Health Organization cannot ultimately be detached from the United Nations, nor the United Nations from questions of international order. We saw this in the Congo.

3

SOME CLUES FROM CHURCH HISTORY

WE go on to indicate very briefly some landmarks in the onward march, as the church proceeded gradually to reintegrate its life with the life of the world around. We shall see how, generally speaking, it dealt with situations one by one as they arrived, sometimes with more success and sometimes with less, now making a perceptible advance and conquering some new area for Christ, now driven back and digging in, now looking more like a bridgehead, now like a hedgehog provisioned from above. We shall see that both the many, who went far in conforming to the world, and the few, who protested and sometimes gave their lives as a ransom for the many, had their indispensable parts to play.

With this picture in mind we shall look once more at the Christian attitude to armaments and war, and finally try to estimate the situation in which our decisions have to be made.

SOME LANDMARKS IN CHURCH HISTORY

The first few landmarks appear in the New Testament itself. First and most important, the church as a universal society transcending barriers of race and culture became possible when the Council of Jerusalem decided that the Gentiles need not keep the Jewish law. The break with Judaism was completed when the Christians escaped to Pella from Jerusalem before the great siege in A.D. 70, but already by that time it was predominantly Gentile. That it lost its minority of practicing Jews may be its first great failure.

The institution of slavery was not and could not be attacked at first; but the justification of slavery, with the slave as an "animated tool," was undermined when St. Paul called Onesimus his son, and bond and free entered the church on the same terms.

The claim of earthly rulers to be divine, or to have absolute autonomy, became impossible when the Christians died rather than worship Caesar.

At first the Christians had no political influence, and only considered governments as pagan authorities demanding the Christian's obedience. The writers of the first three centuries acknowledge that they may serve a good cause, but regard it as out of the question that the Christians should serve as government officials or in the army.[1] The Christians in other words, however much their numbers may have grown, are still "the few," bearing a minority witness, and persecuted or tolerated by "the many."

The conversion of Constantine, who won the decisive battle for possession of the Empire under the sign of the cross, changed all this. Christians could no longer stay detached from the business of government, cultivating personal perfection and criticizing government from outside. The theologians change their tune, and only too soon the Christians are employing the power of the state to put down not only paganism but deviant forms of Christianity.

From this point the church is much more deeply committed to accommodating itself to the world's methods of preserving order and producing wealth, and more committed to generalizing and legislating. The pattern of saving "by many or by few" takes a new shape. On the one hand are the majority, generally conforming to the world; and at its best this movement would express the glory of God in just government, splendid buildings, literature, and artistic achievement of every kind. But there were also always the protesting minorities: ascetics, like monks in the desert or in monasteries; puritanical protestants against pagan customs, such as the iconoclasts in art. The rejection of all Greek and Roman naturalism produced a new and austere type of symbolism which itself became the prevalent fashion in the early Middle Ages. Monasteries, which in the Dark Ages had sent out heroic missionaries to convert the barbarian invaders, preserved the seeds of a cultural life which would eventually expand and civilize the savages. How far the authority and standards of the church can be expanded into the political organization, how far kings and emperors can be required to submit themselves to a spiritual authority, these are the recurring questions of the Middle Ages. The feudal system, in origin the only practicable method of

[1] In fact some Christians did serve as soldiers.

preserving order among barbarians, comes to be seen as a structure through which the whole universe is related to the supreme sovereignty of God.

In this stage it was almost inevitable that the area in which God's kingdom could operate should be identified with Christendom, and only natural that the gospel should be defended and even extended by military operations against the heathen, as in the crusades.

If our general conception is correct, we cannot simply say in any instance that a majority or minority were wrong or right. Rather we must recognize that the effort of the Christian ruler to employ his forces in obedience to his Lord, of the Christian merchant and artist to make the best of both worlds, and of those who embraced holy poverty for the love of God, all had a share in the same Spirit. Each had his own characteristic failures and each produced his own characteristic fruits.

At the height of the Middle Ages, somewhere about the period of St. Thomas Aquinas, it might have seemed as though at last a stable balance had been arrived at. Natural law and natural reason were recognized in their own proper sphere, and above these was the supernatural realm where revelation prevailed. For a minority there was a call to the way of perfection denying this world, and for the majority the way of living in this world without deadly sin and with a prospect of sharing by grace in the joys of the world to come.

This too was premature. Secular arts and secular learning upset the balance and overthrew the too simple scheme. As they began studying the Bible for themselves men discovered how far the hierarchical authority of the church had departed from the simplicity of the primitive gospel.

From this distance we are beginning to see how much the Protestants and Catholics shared, how much of their controversy was a domestic quarrel within the Christian family, and even within the framework of ideas about God and his relation to the world which they both owed to the feudal model. We can also see in the faithful martyrs on both sides the witness of the Holy Spirit by which the whole church still lives, and even in the earnestness of sincere persecutors, a witness to the objectivity of truth as opposed to the too easy tolerance which allows everyone to think what he likes.

But far more important than the domestic quarrel between Protestants and Catholics was the emergence into the full light of day of the spirit of scientific inquiry and the technological revolution which made man for the first time feel that he could indeed become master of this world and determine that he would do so. This conviction was itself a by-product of the Christian conviction that the world could be understood because it is rational and that man has been given authority within it.

In the last three centuries the church in the West, working out from its traditional base in Europe, has been able to exploit the opportunities which the secular revolution offered. The first explorers of the Indies, both east and west, were able to establish the church with the aid of force, so that it has almost everywhere survived to the present day. The extension of European commerce and capitalist exploitation was hardly controlled by the church, whose rules against usury were too rigid. But commerce was followed by government and the opportunities given by both were eagerly seized for the extension of the gospel. Wilberforce and his contemporaries were convinced that "the probable design of Providence in subjecting so large a part of the human race to European government" was the extension of the gospel throughout the world. In fact the vast missionary enterprise of the nineteenth and twentieth centuries would not have happened without the contemporary expansion of commercial and political influence. Meanwhile, the commercial enterprise, when in the hands of moral men, was producing its own philosophy of human betterment, which for the first time had been seen as a practical possibility, and this in turn was reacting with the authoritarian ethics of the church to the benefit of both. By the end of the nineteenth century the more enlightened Christian thinkers had come to terms with the scientist and secular historian, and had satisfied themselves that there was no permanent conflict between the gospel and science properly understood.

Once more, about 1910, it might have seemed as if a stable position had been reached from which there was a good prospect of an unimpeded advance into a world which was more enlightened, better ordered, better fed, more Christian and at peace. Here the church's influence in the world could be seen as exercised largely through devoted and high-principled service in every walk of life, and more particularly as seen from Britain and America in those who volunteered for service overseas to carry the benefits and enlightenment of Western civilization into the darker and more backward parts of the world.

But this also was too simple.

4

THE CHURCH'S ATTITUDE TO WAR

AT the risk of repetition we look back once more, and ask why throughout the greater part of Christian history Christians have borne arms and made war with so little sense of incongruity.

(1) The early Fathers, Justin, Tertullian, Origen, and others, are unanimous in declaring that a Christian cannot bear arms nor function as a magistrate. The church, they say, will struggle against evil, but only with spiritual weapons, and will in fact serve society in general better that way than by compromise. To those who replied that if everyone behaved like that society would fall to pieces, the reply was given that as Christianity spread, the need for forcible restraint of evildoers would become less, and that meanwhile the two methods would work together, until the whole world was Christian. Origen himself, who uses this argument, says that the Christians pray for the success of the Emperor in his "righteous wars." In the view of these theologians not all that is not Christian is wicked. God had sanctioned war in the Old Testament, and the church itself could not have come into being if Rome had not imposed order on the peoples. Here Origen is still speaking as one of "the few."

What did in fact happen was not foreseen.

(2) The fateful step once taken, there were many reasons why war and military service came to be accepted as part of the natural order of things, as inevitable as a judicial system, the accumulation of wealth, and provision for the future. War was a part of the traditional male-dominated way of life, accepted alike by Hebrews, Greeks, and Romans, and going back far behind them all. The male justified himself by fighting, and the female's function was to keep

the home, in some cases even to cultivate the land as well as do the other chores, and to admire her man. To bear arms was the privilege and duty of the free man. In the feudal system this was the primary obligation of every man to his lord, and of the lord to his king. Reinforced by loyalty and the dynastic motive it could be christianized into the beautiful ideal of chivalry.

(3) Savages as they saw them were really savage, barbarian invaders really barbarous, bloody-minded and bad. The Moslem hosts in their view really were the enemies of Christendom. To demand that our partially-civilized ancestors should defend Christendom by mass non-resistance or passive resistance would have been fantastically unrealistic. Small communities of monks or individual missionaries like St. Francis could take that way, backed by an order maintained by other methods, just as they could witness through a holy poverty which could only be practiced by the few.

(4) Enlisted soldiers and mercenaries, native or, like the Swiss Guards, foreign, were bound by a contractual loyalty as sacred to them as any other. And as trade expanded, agreements were entered into with native rulers of other parts, and when these agreements were broken or appeared unjust, commercial morality sanctioned their enforcement by war. In many cases merchants and their families by their existence overseas committed their home governments to a policy first of defense, then of aggression, and finally of annexation. Then the government is recognized *de jure*, and is a legitimate wager of war in its own name, while the natives who resist it are rebels.

(5) Europe in ancient times felt it was defending, and in modern times felt it was extending, a civilized way of life, better than that of the barbarian outsiders or the "natives" whom they conquered. Even when that was not true, they thought it so, and were justified in their own eyes by the fact that their technical competence gave them victory.

The colors of our regiments hanging in our cathedrals and their memorials on the wall show that all this is still part of our image of ourselves.

NATURAL LAW AND THE JUST WAR

The doctrine that there is a natural law of right and wrong which surrounds and supplements the way of Christian love is already implicit in the church's recognition of Caesar. This, and not any specifically Christian doctrine, is the foundation of the theory of the just war as formulated by St. Augustine, St. Thomas, and other theologians in the catholic tradition. It is the most articulate attempt to describe the conditions under which a war can be engaged in by a Christian or any other humane person with an easy conscience.

For a war to be "just" it must

(a) have been undertaken by a lawful authority;

(b) have been undertaken for the vindication of an undoubted right that had been certainly infringed;

(c) be a last resort, all peaceful means of settlement having failed;

(d) offer the possibility of good to be achieved outweighing the evils that war would involve;

(e) be waged with a reasonable hope of victory for justice;

(f) be waged with right intention;

(g) use methods that are legitimate, i.e., in accordance with man's nature as a rational being, with Christian moral principles and international agreements.

The obvious weakness in this whole conception is that in the absence of any competent authority, every nation is a judge in its own cause. Almost every clause contains words which raise the question, "In whose opinion?" Is there any right which someone does not doubt? What government has ever entered a war without persuading itself and its people that the cause was just? And who is to say what is hopeless? Moreover, these standards are heavily (perhaps rightly) weighted against change, for no genuine war of liberation could be started by a "lawful authority."

Some further comments may be made.

The first of the above clauses is specially relevant to the individual citizen's position. The Thirty-seventh Article of Religion of the Church of England assures him that a Christian may bear arms and serve in wars at the command of the magistrate, and this clause similarly assures him that if he is a properly enlisted soldier, killing in battle does not make him guilty of murder. The other clauses in the list are primarily addressed to "princes" or, in modern language, governments, and to citizens insofar as they are responsible for government policy. They do provide some sort of criterion by which public opinion can be guided, and so exercise some control over aggressive statesmen. The seventh condition, however hard it may be to define what the relevant principles are, is at least an acknowl-

23

edgment that not all methods of securing victory are legitimate, and this is something. It was perhaps this condition (*g*), combined with (*d*), that helped to establish the general moral principle that fighting should never be allowed to become disproportionate.

There is however a peculiar difficulty here, for the Christian, once he has enlisted or otherwise committed himself to active participation, must find it extremely hard to withdraw if at some point he thinks the authorities have overstepped the line. This meant agonizing questions for some Christians in the last war, as our own methods became more indiscriminatingly destructive. Do the rules require that a Christian should refuse to take part in a mass bombing raid, or a military leader refuse to give the order for it to be undertaken?

On the other side it may be argued that any teaching that war is just is an invitation to hypocrisy—to moralizing what in fact cannot be moralized and which would much better be accepted, if at all, as sheer necessity. It may be said that the phrase about peaceful means of settlement itself is hypocritical, for every student of politics knows that where vital interests are concerned peaceful settlements are obtained by threat and counterthreat, in which rights and wrongs and power to demand concessions and to refuse them, are inextricably mixed; and as seen by posterity, moral considerations seldom determined anything. An expansion of population; a new technique in industry, navigation or armaments; a new vision of possible wealth for the few or the many; the desire to maintain a lead; the determination to catch up; a new idea of whom the "we" includes; recognized or imagined identities of race, religion or interest; new or surviving focuses for passionate loyalty—these are the hidden or half-hidden forces which make diplomatists dance and armaments build up and armies move.

On this realistic view it would be more honest, and therefore more Christian, to admit that war is always an admission of failure. It may still be the best of two or more bad alternatives; but call it by its proper name. Do not call it just.[2]

A related point may be made. Once we have become persuaded that a given war is being waged to defend or maintain justice, it is easy to come to the erroneous conclusion that it is also a holy war, in which compromise with the enemy is seen as treachery to God; whereas a war which has been undertaken as a frankly bad necessity

---

[2] As a matter of fact, the medieval theologians expounded the rules and explained the word *justum* in such a way as to meet many of these points.

may with more decency be ended without "justice" being achieved or the evildoers punished.

As a further appendix it is worth remembering how often in recent history (e.g., in Ireland and in Cyprus) the "rebels" were at one stage outside the pale, false bearers of bloodstained hands with whom it would be treason to parley; only if they abjured the appeal to force (which in a rebellion begins nearly always as sporadic murder and sabotage) could discussions be entertained. Sooner or later the scene changes. The former rebels are invited to conference, and given all or most of what they had been fighting for. Much of the earlier moralizing is soon forgotten.

More effective by far in mitigating the horrors of war has been the acceptance, mainly since the eighteenth century, of certain human-itarian principles, codified in explicit or implicit conventions, and rarely (and then shamefully) broken by civilized nations: the impar-tiality and invulnerability of the Red Cross, the proper treatment of prisoners of war, the duty sometimes carried out at great risk of rescuing drowning men, friend or enemy, at sea. This last was always subject to the overriding demands of battle, and in submarine war-fare almost went by the board.

Gradually over the ages certain other principles of international law have also developed. Action should not be unnecessarily or unreasonably cruel; reasonable discrimination should be shown be-tween combatants and non-combatants, and between belligerents and neutrals; poisonous weapons should be barred; reprisals (or "protec-tive retribution") taken in retaliation for breaches of these rules should only be on the basis of "an eye for an eye," and not an excuse for abandoning them. All these, however, were more honored in the breach than the observance, and usually according to calculation of which course was the more advantageous.

But can any of these mitigating principles survive a modern all-out war, or any war fought with modern weapons?

5

THE BACKGROUND OF THE PRESENT CRISIS

1914-1939

WHERE we are now is in the aftermath of the convulsive break-up of the pre-1914 liberal-imperial-mercantile balance of power. It is as well to remind ourselves at the outset that though we date the breakup from 1914, in the previous fifty years Britain had fought innumerable small wars in the consolidation of the Empire, and in certain areas, such as the northwest frontier of India, may be said to have been continuously at war. The only one of these which seriously worried the conscience of many British citizens was the South African War, partly because it was against white men.

War broke out in 1914 because the long accumulated fears and ambitions on both sides became uncontrollable, because some powerful people wanted war, and because even those who did not want it made miscalculations.

It is at least a tenable view that World War I could have ended sooner in a negotiated peace if the Allies had been less deeply committed to the moralistic line. "Germany must acknowledge her guilt and the guilty must be punished." If this was the whole truth, all compromise was necessarily a betrayal of justice.

The Treaty of Versailles, which began with the enforced confession of war guilt and committed itself to the impossible program of making Germany pay for the war, had the support not only of Lloyd George and Clemenceau, true representatives of their bitterly vengeful electorates, but also of the highly moral President Wilson. But along with this went an outburst of idealistic confidence in the League of Nations, which was to make the world safe for democracy and end the era of wars forever. Only a few far-sighted cynics remembered the Congress of Vienna and the high ideals of the then Czar Alexander I of Russia, and how soon the realities, political and economic rivalries, reasserted themselves.

In this period the churches uncritically reflected the majority opinion. For the most part they blessed the war while it was on, and made no effective protest when the blockade was maintained after the armistice.

But this is not the whole story. For the first time, in the postwar period, Christians took the lead in a program of relief, which made no distinction between guilty and not guilty, former enemies and former friends. The churches became strong if not always discriminating advocates of the League of Nations. Leaders of the churches forged new links with one another which were later to stand a still more serious strain, and helped to re-establish the connection between the missionaries of enemy nationality and their adherents overseas.

The churches did not at that stage concern themselves greatly with the tiresome details of international politics. They trusted, perhaps too naively, in the effect of personal links and better understanding, as making war less likely. But they were not wrong in believing that whatever might happen, it was their duty and privilege to make friends.

The long drawn out and mainly futile attempt to limit armaments by negotiation seemed to show that disarmament was a consequence of peace with justice rather than a means of attaining it. While the nations were still at bottom unable to trust one another, the balancing of relative strengths and proposals for the gradual or dramatically sudden scaling down of arms were really maneuvers in the old game. The Kellogg Pact was an unrealistic attempt to achieve peace by a gesture.

Disillusionment followed in due course. Perhaps the majority had always hoped that having won the war, they should now enjoy the fruits of victory in a life of pleasure. The General Strike and the Great Depression made them wonder what would have been worse if we had lost. The poor had been good enough for cannon fodder, but when they were no longer needed for that, they were free to rot. The idealists began to wonder whether the League had failed. The reaction of some of them, including some of the best and most consciously Christian in their intentions, was to despair of the nicely calculated less and more of negotiation, and demand a short cut to peace. The pacifist movement appealed to two classes of people. There were those who could remember the first war, and those who could not. The former had fought, or knew those who had fought and died; they felt they had been let down, and they were not prepared to be had again, nor to see their sons sacrificed to no purpose. Others, and these the majority, had never seen war. They had never known what it means to risk the loss of everything and life itself. War was something that statesmen made and young men paid for, and they did not believe in it. But there was more to it than that. The Christians among them, the most sincerely Christian, argued, "The world's way of making peace has been tried, and we will try Christ's way. For sixteen centuries now, Christians have compromised with the world, have professed, perhaps sincerely, to be seeking peace and serving justice, and have got numerous wars instead. Let others have their wars if they will, but don't claim the sanction of Christ for them, and don't ask us to have anything to do with them."

Meanwhile the Russian revolution was passing into its nationalistic-aggressive phase; the Germans and Italians had each found the focus and mouthpiece for their neurotic frustrations, and were visibly preparing for war.

In this context it is difficult to resist the conclusion that the main political effect of the pacifist movement, and of the unwillingness to face unpleasant facts which many shared who did not share its Christian principles, was to inhibit the government from a vigorous presentation of the facts, and to induce it to begin rearmament too little and too late.

More representative leaders in the churches had meanwhile given a great deal of thought to general principles and the theology of international affairs, and broadly speaking two schools of thought emerged: a more liberal, represented mainly in the Anglo-Saxon countries, and a more pessimistic, represented mainly by the Continental theologians. Both have a share in responsibility for the tragedy. The former were to blame in not being realistic enough in recognizing hard facts. We were too comfortably assured of our own sweet reasonableness and trusted that others too, even Hitler, would prove to be reasonable in the end. The latter were responsible also by acquiescing too readily in the division between this world in which the Christian must expect to go on sinning and the world of Christ where he is justified by faith alone. The Anglo-Saxon hoped, even against the evidence, that if he did God's will, as he set himself to do, with some hope at any rate of approximating to it, all things would work together for good. The Continental knew that he could not do God's will and was ill-prepared to see that some courses of action were more damnable than others.

These various influences made the program of "appeasement" (in spite of the fact that it was made at other peoples' expense) seem right at the time to many Christians and other people of goodwill, and if it had not been first tried, the war, when it came, would have been less obviously necessary and we should have entered it with a troubled conscience.

1939-1946

Judged by the criteria of the just war as given above, the Allies could be satisfied that resistance to Hitler was indeed legitimate, and many who till 1939 had been pacifists came to see this and joined up. Others maintained their personal protest but served in ambulances or in civilian work.

The Many and the Few. The few continued to give their minority witness most effectively if their service was not less sacrificial than service in the armed forces. The Quakers and others who had persistently taken this position did gain for themselves the respect of people in all countries, and were able to take a lead in relief and reconciliation as opportunity offered. If our general view is correct, it is good that the few should witness in this manner.

But the many, the majority who supported the war, were too little sensitive to the increasing ruthlessness of our methods. Only a few courageous voices were raised against mass bombing and such incidents as the burning of Hamburg. Very few refused to take part in the rejoicing after the bombing of Hiroshima; hardly any protested against the demand for total surrender. This is the danger of going with the majority. One is swept along when any criticism of the majority point of view is felt to be disloyal, and this is most of all the case in time of war or near war, when it is almost impossible to get a true picture of the facts and the emotional strain is great. In many other respects also, as the war proceeded the criteria of the just war seemed to point the other way. In 1940 who was to say whether further resistance was hopeless? When Russia came in, her accession to the alliance was welcomed as a sheer necessity if victory was to be won, but whether explicitly or not, the objectives for which the war was being fought became increasingly compromised from that moment. So the entry of Russia was welcomed by some as offering a hope of prolonged cooperation in a socialist future, but feared by others as an alliance of incompatibles which could not last.

In such a confused situation degrees of guilt and innocence are past judging by human standards. The individual soldier or airman had his orders. Prayers were said before the airplane took off which dropped the A-bomb on Hiroshima, and who is to say that they were blasphemous? There is a long tradition that in war all that is necessary for victory is justified, and this may be accepted as a legitimate defense for those who acquiesce in ruthlessness. Nevertheless there was widespread uneasiness, and some explicit protest, as by some American scientists.

SINCE 1946

The postwar settlement made less moral claims for itself than the Treaty of Versailles. It was mainly a recognition of fact, as where Germany was divided along the lines of military occupation when the fighting stopped. Very soon the weak states on the eastern frontier were swallowed up by the U.S.S.R. with no more moral justification than was available for Hitler's invasion of Poland. The satellite countries were not rescued by the West, not because they did not deserve it, but because they could not be. The United Nations, compared with the League of Nations, was less idealistic, less given to long term hopes, but on occasion showed itself more competent to deal with concrete situations. It remained, at the worst, a forum in which the conflicting powers could state their cases in words and, as things developed, neither of the two great blocs could afford to ignore the mass of uncommitted opinion represented by the African and Asian nations. Compared with the period between the wars, the period from 1945 to the present time has been marked by a more empirical and careful and step by step approach to problems both internal and external. The everpresent and increasing possibility of atomic annihilation has exercised a restraining effect all round on military and political adventures. Whereas after the first war the Americans had thought that they could call it a day when the war was won, and pull out, after the second they knew that this was impossible. The impatience which prompted some to demand the bombing of China or Russia or both in order to get it over with was not allowed to have its way. Both sides continued to appeal to moral principles and to represent themselves as the Free World or the People's Democracies respectively, but neither side could afford to let its policies be guided by its professed principles. Under the threat of unlimited destruction, positive action in any direction was scaled down, and this applied to both sides equally, for deterrence had become mutual.

6

THE VALLEY OF DECISION

"Multitudes, multitudes,
   in the valley of decision!
For the day of the LORD is near
   in the valley of decision."
                    Joel 3:14

WHERE WE ARE NOW

IN 1939 the white races, who traditionally had belonged to Christendom, and who had led the world in technical advance, still held sway over vast areas in Asia and Africa, and decisions which affected their populations for good or evil were taken in the West. Their resources were exploited, their labor was mobilized, their landscapes were transformed in response to the demands of the markets in London and New York. Most of these people are now politically independent, relatively backward in technology but determined to catch up. In the long run the future of the world may depend on the success or failure of both parties in adjusting themselves to this unprecedented situation, in which neither commercial morality nor condescending benevolence is a sufficient guide to conduct.

Meanwhile the landscape is dominated by the two great power blocs ranged against one another. Neither is monolithic, nor necessarily permanent. Each has the power at present utterly to destroy the other, at the cost of almost certainly being destroyed itself. The uncommitted nations have their own rivalries, and are tempted to ally themselves with one side or the other, or to seek safety by playing them off against each other.

The Bible and subsequent history suggest that the creative line of divine providence may not lie with either of the great powers or with any combination of them. But they, and we, are certainly within God's control.

There is no practicable way back into a viable world without scientific knowledge and applied technology; any relapse would be into a far worse state than medieval simplicity or any known variety of primitive barbarism. Since God is in control, there must be a way forward.

In a world unified by technology, where none can live without the services of the rest, the direction of advance must point toward a united world; and how to achieve this while preserving the essential freedoms for individuals and communities is the long-term constructive project which should engage the enthusiastic support of all men of good will. Christians can bring to it the added assurance that it is in accordance with God's will. In this realm the church may reasonably expect to give a lead, following up in new and much more costly ways the humanitarian efforts which it has undertaken all over the world in the last 150 years.

But more particularly, Christians on many occasions have had to stand as minorities for the rights of the individual conscience; and if, as we have claimed, the Holy Spirit works through minorities and majorities held together in charity, we shall not be surprised or distressed if we find that on some crucial issues we are still divided. For part of what we stand for as Christian, and part of what Western democracy in the providence of God has stood for, and stands for still, is the right of minorities to be respected, and of majorities to have their way.

Christian Decision and Particular Decisions

The first and fundamental decision which every Christian has taken in principle, but has to reassert day by day, is this: Is my primary and overriding allegiance to Christ? If I see what is the Christian thing to do, if as far as I can see a certain course is Christian, do I promise in advance to follow it? I may fail, and often do, but do I then repent and pray to do better?

The second decision follows from the first. Do I acknowledge that I owe an overriding loyalty to my fellow Christians everywhere? Are they, for me, the ultimate "we" to which I belong?

And thirdly, is the Christian tradition, are Christian principles, to have a first claim on my loyal assent? If so, this commits me to attaching weight to the guidance of leaders of Christian thought; and in a divided church, to the leaders of my own communion. I may have to differ from them in the name of Christ, but if I do, it must be in his name and no other.

Unless we can say that this is what we know ought to be the case, and what at bottom we want to be the case, the particular decisions we make are not really Christian decisions at all.

PARTICULAR DECISIONS

These are relative to contemporary facts, dependent on our judgment of the facts, and so are always provisional and liable to revision.

(1) *The Church as "The Many."* The first decision is still general. Is the church right or wrong in behaving as "the many"? This does not mean, Does it claim to be a majority of the whole people? It means that it accepts the position it has usually had in Western Europe and America since the time of Constantine, as part of the accepted order, committed to political responsibility, with all that we have seen that that implies.

That this is still the case is the presupposition of the majority of all the churches in Britain and the U.S.A. There are certain groups which in principle say, "No." They think that the church was guilty of the great betrayal in the age of Constantine. And there are others who, faced with the consequences of cooperation with the state, at some point or other say, "No. On this point, if on no other, I must refuse assent."

A few groups, and a few individuals, have refused assent to the economic system (as far as they could); others have refused to appeal to the state's ordering of justice. Many more—though no great communion except the Quakers—have refused to take responsibility for the state's use of armed force in international affairs. This is the position of pacifists as such, and of the Campaign for Nuclear Disarmament insofar as national defense policy contemplates the use of or possession of nuclear weapons for any purpose whatever.

The standpoint of this pamphlet is that this is a mistaken decision. Reasons will be given for this, but meanwhile it should be clear that we do not for a moment deny the right of others to their opinion. We ought to be sensitive to the reasons which make them differ from us. For our part we are committed to accepting responsibility as Christians for the use of power at every level. We realize (from our knowledge of history and our own experience) how dangerous is the way of consent to "Caesar's" claims. We may easily conform too much to the world's way of thinking; and if once we lose our power of independent criticism we are back at the idolatry of Caesar which the martyrs died to break.

(2) *The National Loyalty of the Church.* The second decision is this: As Christians we are committed to aiming at the good of all people wherever and whoever they may be; there is no one to whom we have no obligation. Does this mean that we have equal duties to all, or have we a special duty towards our own country and to our own friends? The Christian involved in society must surely recognize obligation in a series of concentric circles and not ignore his immediate neighbors or his natural friends in the name of a general benevolence ("telescopic philanthropy," in Dickens' phrase). Often the best way of helping these is to do our usual job well. Moreover, any country can only effectively help other people if it maintains its own life healthy and effective. Keeping one's own country orderly and safe may well be the first step and the best step toward securing order and safety for anyone else. To build up and maintain economic and other power is the prerequisite for using power for anyone else's good. We have already seen how in previous times, the Holy Spirit has made use of economic and political opportunities; and this course is also sanctioned by the biblical pattern of God's working, e.g., through and in Israel first in order that Israel might have something to give.

There is a proper place in individual life and in the life of a nation for enlightened self-interest. We all accept this in private life; it would be unrealistic to profess otherwise in regard to the nation.

We may then frankly admit that in thinking of international affairs and defense we include the safety and welfare of our own country. But it also follows that no people whatever are outside the pale. We have obligations toward them all. This may seem obvious, but it cannot be taken for granted, for in various periods of history primitive people have been treated as less than human, and even now it is too easy to wipe out from our minds whole masses of people as somehow mattering less than we do ourselves.

The conclusion here would seem to be that Christians, like everyone else, are committed to the tiresome process of accommodation and compromise and the balance of rights and duties. There is no short cut by ignoring our obligations to those who are far off or to those who are near.

(3) *People and Ideologies.* Which for the Christian are primary and real, people or ideologies? The answer must be that people are the objects of God's love; people separately and in groups. We are told to love our brethren and our enemies. Therefore the Christian must try at all times to think in terms of people, and not of abstractions such as communism, atheism, imperialism, etc. We must use our imaginations to see the people behind the images which the nations present to the world. We can take opportunities by travel. We can take them by getting to know the foreigners in our midst. We can read and listen to the radio and watch television.

Christian history shows the horrors of ideological warfare even within Christendom, but witnesses also to the fact of friendship across ideological barriers. The principalities and powers over which Christ won his victory are perhaps those very abstractions and "isms," idols and images which prevent the real meeting of people. If so, he won his victory by refusing to work according to their scheme, and by meeting publicans and sinners, Pharisees and Roman soldiers, and by meeting everyone as himself. We should therefore be grateful for the many books in recent years which have helped us to see what warfare (and atomic warfare) means in terms of what it does to people, and in general to look over the garden wall and see how our neighbors live.

(4) *God and the West.* In the line-up of the two great blocs, can God's cause, or the Christian cause, or Christian civilization, be identified with the cause of the West?

We call ourselves the free world, but the "free world" includes autocratic governments, and colored and colonial peoples still in subjection; freedom is limited by economic pressures; the great inequalities of power have even meant freedom to exploit the weak. Pakistan, Turkey, and Iran do not even profess the Christian faith, and we are all beset by the prevalent materialism and continual suggestion that man's life consists in the multitude of things which he possesses.

The "people's democracies" also include satellite nations held down by force, such as invaded Hungary and Tibet; relatively efficient control of thought by propaganda; ruthless planned economy and direction of labor; but also many signs of genuine enthusiasm for public service and a willing acceptance of discipline such as Western people have accepted only in time of war. The Russians and Chinese share the West's convictions about the value of material things, but believe that their possession can only be achieved by ruthless planning. In the light of their own history they may be right.

On both sides the church as representing a colony of the kingdom of heaven must be at odds with contemporary society at many points. In the Western world it can still, we believe, cooperate at many points with "Caesar." In the communist countries the Christian witness is more restricted. It witnesses against dogmatic atheism and the idolatry of the state by continuing to worship God, and the Christian retains, though maybe at his peril, a sense of his unity in Christ with us on the other side of the barrier.

The political climate of the West is more congenial to the church, the climate of the East more rigorous. It is difficult for different reasons to be truly Christian in either, though not impossible.

It follows:

(*a*) The Western line-up is not a defense of Christianity.

(*b*) There is no evidence to suggest that a surrender to Communism would mean the death of the Christian faith or the end of Christian practice.

(*c*) The defense of the West is not a holy war, and any movement toward compromise or co-existence is not a betrayal of Christianity or a denial of God.

We retain our own conviction that the Western way of life, with more tolerance, with more respect for the individual conscience, with more impartial justice, with more opportunity for free enterprise, with less control from above and greater reliance on individual self-discipline, with a greater reverence for truth undistorted by propaganda, is a better way of life than the alternative of rigorous control from above with all that that implies. In defending ourselves we defend these values too. There is the more reason that in defending ourselves and our own way of life because it is ours and because we think it contains intrinsically good elements, we should not use methods which would betray the values we think we stand for.

(5) *The Thought Barrier and the Cold War.* It has been well said that survival in the nuclear age depends on being able to break through the "thought barrier." When the possibilities of action for good or evil were severely limited, remoter effects could for practical purposes be ignored; people inaccessible or unheard of raised no problems. Now peace is indivisible, feeding the hungry is indivisible, civilization is indivisible, as are technical knowledge and the use or

abuse of it for war or peace. Survival, if it is to be attained, is indivisible too.

To realize this means to think and speak habitually as members of a society with open edges, as members of a nation whose sovereignty is already severely limited. Those who are with us, and those who are against us, as we see things now, are all together with us in a common danger and faced with a common opportunity. In the nuclear age the last barriers to mutual involvement are down. To realize this is to disown in principle the concept and the habits of the cold war, and to be committed increasingly to a one-world view.

Beyond defense, disarmament; along with disarmament, *détente*; beyond co-existence, mutual help; beyond preventing aggression, cooperation in a common order: these are the demands of the nuclear age.

Mankind has come so far by ceaseless struggle. There is built into our nature a combative element which has its links with love, so that we are never happier, never more fully alive, than when we stand shoulder to shoulder with loyal friends to fight a common enemy. Thus a common danger aids consolidation, increases capacity for effort, and generates self-sacrifice. Millions found this to be true in time of war; tyrants have often exploited it to consolidate their power.

The cold war freezes this state of mind, and fixes it as a habitual framework which determines everything. But the real enemies—annihilation, disease, starvation, premature death, the loss of those we love, hatred, malice and all uncharitableness, ignorance, hard-heartedness, and willful blindness—threaten all alike. It is the devil's device to make us attach to our human opponents the hatred and unwearying suspicion of which he is the proper object, and to worship him in the cast-iron frozen image of the cold war.

DEFENSE POLICY AND THE PREVENTION OF WAR

We come at long last to the specific issue of defense policy. We are to concentrate here on the prevention of war, rather than spreading ourselves on all the other things which we might do to bring about a better world, because the prevention of open large scale war is the first and indispensable condition of anything else whatever. It should not engage our whole attention, but it is the Number One priority. It is also the interest of all people without exception.

There is no need to enlarge on the destructive power of nuclear weapons. We know, the Russians know, we all know, that full scale, all-out war must be prevented. At present both parties are committed to a policy of "mutual deterrence" which may be defined as follows. Each has a stock of nuclear warheads sufficient to obliterate the other, and is trying to make their means of delivery so invulnerable that a single knock-out blow would be impossible. This is admittedly a dangerous situation, in which war might break out by accident or by miscalculation; but both these dangers are likely to be progressively reduced as means of warning and obtaining accurate information are improved, and as the means of retaliation become more truly invulnerable. The trend of weapon-development on both sides toward the production of such invulnerable weapons as the submarine-launched Polaris missile should therefore be welcomed and not resented.

Can a Christian support this policy of mutual deterrence at the strategic level? Here is a summary of the arguments as they seem to be presented by each side.

(1) *The Case for Deterrence*

(*a*) If it is clear that an attack with megaton weapons will be answered with megaton weapons, such an attack will be so liable to become suicidal that neither side will risk it.

(*b*) If one side retained the power of ultimate destruction and the other side did not, the one which had the advantage might be tempted to try it out, with terrible results.

(*c*) The side which retained power could practice continual blackmail.

(*d*) If one side were to lose or surrender its deterrent capacity, its adversary would be in a position to attack or threaten other powers, and ultimately nuclear war would come just the same.

(*e*) If Christian or pacifist pressure so weakened the power of the West to retaliate that the U.S.S.R. did try it out, we should in part be responsible for the result.

(*f*) If war is thus avoided, both the potential belligerents and the neutrals will benefit.

(*g*) Such a position of mutual deterrence at this level also offers the best present hope of restraint being exercised at the lower levels of fighting, and thus avoiding both "escalation" and another prolonged conventional world war.

(*h*) Military stalemate offers a position which can be used to obtain agreements on disarmament and other issues.

(2) *The Case against Deterrence*

(*a*) Deterrence involves assenting to the possibility of killing millions of men, women, and children in retaliation, should the bomb be used against ourselves. Can the Christian possibly assent to this?

(*b*) The compromise sometimes suggested, that we should possess the means of deterrence but determine never to use it, is unrealistic. If it were known we should never use it, it would lose its power to deter; if it were not known, but secretly agreed (by whom?) that we should never use it, we should still be morally committed to the intention of using it.

(*c*) Such an attitude toward our fellow creatures must inevitably prejudice our efforts to foster trust, reconciliation, and settlement.

(*d*) The appalling risk of accidents. Deterrence depends on crediting our opponents with steady nerves, good judgment, and sufficiently accurate information.

In the first edition of this pamphlet, published in Britain in 1961, the particular problems facing Britain and the British government at that time were in view, and the writer had the assistance of some who were intimately acquainted with the details of policy. Accordingly there followed a section in which the following points were made:

(1) The possession of the "ultimate deterrent" by both the U.S.A. and the U.S.S.R. offered the best prospect available at the moment of preventing a world-wide war, which must be the first priority. Unilateral nuclear disarmament was more dangerous than the precarious "balance of terror."

(2) An invulnerable capacity to retaliate would make a "first strike" less likely to be successful and less attractive.

(3) The reliance by the West on nuclear superiority and by the U.S.S.R. on conventional superiority was making agreed disarmament in either field more difficult.

(4) The inferiority of the West in conventional weapons, particularly in Europe, meant that the West was committed in certain circumstances to be the first to use nuclear weapons. This was an intolerable position to be in.

(5) Once *any* nuclear weapons had been used, the danger of escalation was immensely increased. The West should, therefore, strengthen its conventional armaments and bring them up to date. This would not necessarily mean trying to match the Russians man for man.

(6) Britain's own nuclear deterrent (estimated at five percent of the total available to the West) had no independent value. Britain should continue to support NATO, but could do this more effectively by scrapping or sharing its nuclear weapons and spending the money so saved on strengthening its conventional forces. To withdraw from NATO or to refuse to cooperate with the nuclear forces of the U.S.A. would make large scale war more likely.

(7) In the field of massive deterrents, if each side has enough for effective retaliation, there is no point in having more, and parity becomes irrelevant. Thus even in the context of this policy it would seem to be common sense for both sides to call a halt at least to the manufacture of any more fissile material for military purposes.

(8) Various steps were suggested for the limitation and control of various types of weapons, agreed zones within which they should not be deployed, and so on.

(9) The purpose of the deterrent must be purely the prevention of war and never the waging of it. If deterrence failed, no human purpose could be achieved by continuing war with nuclear weapons and a halt must be called at whatever the cost. We should not, at this stage, press our governments to state openly in advance how far they would go before calling a halt. We should, however, demand assurance on the general principle of no all-out total war in any circumstances, or indeed any war disproportionate to the issue at stake.

Since 1961, little if any progress has been made along the lines of the above suggestions. But much has taken place to change the scene. So far, war between the great powers has been avoided. That the Cuba crisis did not lead to it may be credited in part to the nuclear deterrent. France and China are developing their own nuclear weapons—France expects to have its own H-bomb by 1970. The Moscow Treaty on the cessation of nuclear testing above ground was a positive achievement which it seemed at one time might be followed up by an agreement also on underground tests, as the means of distant detection were improved and "on site" inspection became less important. But neither France nor China is a party to the treaty, the Geneva negotiations on nonproliferation have so far borne no fruit, and there are hints that other powers may soon develop or acquire nuclear weapons of their own. Even India has been tempted, but so far has not fallen, and in July, 1966, was proposing a new initiative by the UN.

None of the old trouble spots has been decisively cleared, and some new ones have arisen. None of the small wars or war-like incidents has escalated, but there has not been and is not peace. The U.S.S.R. and China have so far had only partial success in promoting anarchy in Africa.

The feeling is gaining ground that the main area of danger is no longer in Europe, and that in spite of the continuing problems of Berlin and divided Germany the West may have over-insured against an overt act of war in Europe. The falling out of Russia and China, and signs of increasing restiveness among the satellite nations of Europe suggest that the conception of a world divided between two solid power blocs, which dominated our thinking in 1961, may be going out of date. President de Gaulle's independent approach to Russia and his partial disengagement from NATO point the same way, as do the beginnings of an Afro-Asian line-up against the "white man."

The nature of the war in Vietnam is raising in the consciences of many the question posed at the end of chapter four. Counter-village bombing with conventional weapons may feel as indiscriminate at the receiving end as counter-city bombing with nuclear weapons. It is important that the consciences which were shocked by Guernica, partially hardened by the obliteration bombing of World War II, and reawakened into horror by Hiroshima and Nagasaki, should not once more be hardened by familiarity. The distinction between the intentional killing of civilians and the unintended results of an operation directed at a military target must never be lost sight of. But it is terribly hard to make it effective in bombing from the air, and the "principle of proportionality" may be nearly impossible to apply.

Added to all this are the potential dangers of the space race and the exploitation of outer space for espionage and eventually, it may be, for destructive purposes as well.

Discussions of British policy were, and still more are, influenced by our awareness of our comparative economic weakness and strategic vulnerability, and consequently of our ultimate dependence, however much disguised, on the U.S.A. We have taken for granted hitherto that for practical purposes the resources of the U.S.A. were unlimited. But there are signs that even these are feeling the strain.

These developments will seem to some to vindicate the arguments used in 1961 and to counsel further patient efforts toward international agreement under the umbrella of terror. Others will see in the increasing dangers a call for a total reversal of policy, and particularly for Christians to dissociate themselves once and for all from threats or use of force which is becoming more and more uncontrollable.

We have tried to show our American friends the view as seen from here. From where they are it is bound to look somewhat different. But it is the same landscape. We can agree, as we consult together, on many features of it, and on the general direction in which, from our different positions, we can move. It is our hope and prayer that this account of how we in Britain have tried to make our decisions will help Americans to make their own.

The above are some of the considerations to be borne in mind when discussing defense policy in the technical sense. We do not profess to lay down a policy in detail. Only the government with the help of its expert advisers can do that. The situation may change any day, with a new lead from the United States, with a new approach by the U.S.S.R., with a new weapon invented or a new warning technique, or a change in the economic situation.

But we are entitled to demand that we be told the truth. We do not expect security on the cheap, and are prepared to give up some of our luxuries and some of our comforts if we are persuaded that that is the price of peace and the hope of a better world. We are entitled to leadership from those we have helped to put in power, and to be told in what direction we are being led, and to protest with all the power at our command if we think we are being misled. We have seen too much of ignorant complacency alternating with moments of panic. We demand to be treated as adults.

We demand a much stronger lead in the common fight against hunger, disease, ignorance, and want, not for our own sake, not as an insurance against the spread of communism, but because these things are bad. And we believe that if we are in earnest much more can be done in this way, even without cutting our expenditure on arms; but only if we are in earnest where it hurts.

It is the government's business to give us as far as possible what we really want. As long as we want what we cannot have, i.e., to go on enjoying our present advantages without really caring for the rest, we have only ourselves to blame.

How much do we care for the peace of India, of Africa, of the world?

7

PRINCIPLES AND COMPROMISE

ONCE more, and for the last time, we ask ourselves: Are we compromising too much? Are we yielding to expediency instead of following clear principles?

Those who say "Yes" will attack us for opposite reasons. Some will say, "You have pitched your aims too low. You have suggested again and again that there are rights and wrongs on both sides, and if anything have weighted the scales in favor of our opponents. But if we fight at all, we fight, not only or mainly for ourselves, but for truth, justice, and freedom, for the common virtues and the human decencies, even if with an eye on Pakistanis and Indians and our own Jews and humanists you will not call these values Christian. Communism is the negation of all we stand for, as civilized human beings and as Christians. 'For God and the right!' We could not fight for less. 'Let justice be done, though the heavens fall.' That is no rhetorical exaggeration, but even so we cannot compromise."

This is a heroic attitude which any man, ancient pagan or modern Christian, may take up if he sees the picture so. But to keep his conscience clear he has no right to pull the heavens down on those who do not agree with him. He is not entitled to commit his country to the flames, nor yet to annihilate against their will the victims of a regime which in his judgment is unjust. In choosing to be one of a faithful few he must contrive that at least the immediate consequences of his stand fall on himself and those who choose to stand with him. It is irresponsible to sabotage attempts at compromise which are supported by the majority.

A parallel position is taken on the other wing. These too refuse to compromise—they refuse to use weapons to defend the right.

Neither can they presume to force their country to follow the way of non-resistance, nor by their opposition sabotage its efforts to defend itself by arms.

Both groups, if they will, can be in fellowship with the majority, who want both peace and justice, but neither at any price.

The churches and the Christians who take the middle line must be at most the fellow-travelers, never the prisoners or mere camp-followers and apologists, of the popular will. They must continually keep in mind the object of the exercise, which is the good of all mankind; first, the prevention of war, second, the promotion of a real and lasting peace, and the achievement of a relatively fair and stable adjustment of rival claims and interests, including our own. They must constantly beware of ideology, which substitutes abstractions for people, and idolatry, which gives full allegiance to any authority other than God, as his will appears to be revealed to them day by day.

Providence and Foresight

In conclusion, we must ask ourselves, and make ourselves give an answer: What do we as Christians bring that is unique to the decision of these questions and the dealing with these matters?

The short answer is: We have faith in God's providence. And having said that, we notice that of this also there is an inverted reflection in the communist's creed. He too believes, as many in the West do not, that there is a power at work in history which is in the end irresistible, and that being right is being in line with that.

For us the clue to the nature and purpose of that providence is given in the Bible, with Jesus Christ as its center. We have seen there how God continually brought good out of evil; how the faithfulness of the few could be used to save the many (and yet the many had to be there to attach the few to earth); how often disaster meant fresh opportunity; how a small people and a feeble one could count for more in the history of mankind than the mighty powers of the world. We have seen that the people who obeyed God were employed as partners in his purpose, and how even those who did not obey were made unwittingly to serve it too.

We have seen that the pattern of death and resurrection, of failure and fresh start, has been repeated again and again. We have seen that the reward of faithfulness is the grace of further faithfulness, and the privilege not of comfort but of service. We have seen that for the church, as for the nations, there is no permanent halting place, but always in the decay of the old order a challenge to new adventure.

We can, if we wish, take the story back, as Teilhard de Chardin does, to the beginning of life, and trace a similar pattern all the way.

At the center is the death and resurrection of the Lord; and there is our guarantee that love and life, not death and hatred, have the last word. It happened here, in this world; and in this world, therefore, love and life have the last word.

God made man his vice-regent on earth; and in spite of our abuse of it, he has not withdrawn his mandate. In the mighty works of Christ we have a preview of a world obeying God in man his representative; in the partial victories of the church we see a further installment of the power which brings good out of evil. And in the last four centuries we have seen mankind growing up more and more rapidly, behaving (and misbehaving) in a more nearly adult and responsible way, till we suddenly find ourselves with the keys of life and death in our hands.

We have been necessarily most concerned with our common danger. But we can also look forward, again as Chardin teaches us to do, with solid grounds for hope. Already there are signs of a new dawn: in the constructive applications of science to increase the production of food, in spontaneous expressions of good will all round the world in times of natural or man-made disaster, in the welfare agencies sponsored by the UN, in the enthusiastic response of young people in many countries to opportunities of service, in the fellowship of science and research (hampered but not destroyed by national rivalries), in a new and wider effort to understand and appreciate the points of view and convictions of others in religion and behavior. In sport, in art, in music, in aspiration, and even in language, a one-world culture is on its way.

The common danger is also common opportunity.

It is our faith, no more and no less than the ultimate faith of Christians, that God is faithful, and his good will cannot fail. Whether *we* are faithful is the question; if we are not, he is able to raise up others to take over. And for us to be faithful means to grapple faithfully with the facts (his facts); neither to hanker after the past and wish we were not where we are, applying the old formulas blindly in our different situation, nor trying to save our souls (as if we could!) by refusing to become involved with the world. Christians are like salt, which works only in solution. Christian holiness is not the sterile absence of infection, hermetically sealed; it is detergent and antiseptic, which functions where dirt is.

It has been said that Marxism is a Christian heresy, and indeed the communist shares much of this belief, not least in the dialectic between opposites which we have borrowed in expounding it. If once he sees that people are more real than the system and more worthy of reverence, he may come to believe, as his ancestors did, that Person and not Process is the most adequate image of the Ultimate Power. Perhaps he will see this, if we insist on caring for him as a person, meeting him, listening to him, understanding him as a person of like passions with ourselves. Perhaps we shall really believe it too, if we listen to him when he tells of the places in which, as he sees it, we have failed to treat him, and people of other races, as people worthy of reverence. This is hardest to achieve with the statesmen, who more than their followers are the slaves of ideology, but no iron curtain is love-proof.

The old world in which wars between nations were possible is obsolete, but we still have to live with the menace of total destruction. We do our best to ward it off, according to our varying lights and partial judgments. If we do come safely through to a less menacing landscape, it will be of God's mercy, who was able to use the wrath of man, and the fears of man, and the sparks of light and love which enlighten every man, and so to save by love *and* fear.

"Our God whom we serve is able to deliver us from the burning furnace. But if not . . . O King . . . we will not serve your gods or worship the golden image which you have set up." So said the Three Holy Children to King Nebuchadnezzar.

We do not believe the worst will happen. But if it did, in the moment of annihilation we should still be found believing, refusing to hate, refusing to despair. If not here, in this rebellious province of his universe, yet "somewhere else," as using an image we must say, God would still be love, and light, and life. Already I know that in this world any day may be my last, and one day will be. But beyond that are resurrection and immortal life.

In its earliest and most formative period the church lived in the expectation of an imminent end. It learned to live each day as if its last. What those first Christians really cared for was God's kingdom and his righteousness. And so they referred each day's duty to the immediate judgment of the Lord; they were modest (even St. Paul was modest!) in the scales of their planning; they learned to take the next step, and the next one after that. So all we have to do is to bring out of the bag the secret which the church has always had, of living hopefully when the future is obscure. We plan for the future responsibly, knowing that the best plans often go wrong. We do not pin our final hopes on their success. We shall not think the battle is won if the danger recedes, nor yet if the world state comes. Nor shall we despair if the prospect darkens yet more. We will not despair, and we will not hate. In faith and hope and love (God help us!) we will do our best, along with anyone who will join us, or let us join them, on those terms.

For Further Reading

ON THE BIBLICAL AND HISTORICAL BACKGROUND

HESCHEL, ABRAHAM J. *The Prophets.* New York: Harper, 1962. An interpretation of the ethical impulse of the Old Testament.

CAIRD, GEORGE B. *Jesus and the Jewish Nation.* London: Athlone Press, 1965. Stresses Jesus' sense of social responsibility.

MCNEILL, JOHN T. *Christian Hope for World Society.* Chicago: Willett, Clark, 1937. A history of Christian social thought and action.

BAINTON, ROLAND H. *Christian Attitudes toward War and Peace.* Nashville: Abingdon, 1960. An historical study.

TOOKE, JOAN. *The Just War in Aquinas and Grotius.* London: S.P.C.K., 1965. A major scholarly study of the development of this concept.

ON THE CONTEMPORARY PROBLEM

KEE, HOWARD C. *Making Ethical Decisions.* Philadelphia: Westminster, 1957.

LONG, EDWARD LEROY. *Conscience and Compromise: An Approach to Protestant Casuistry.* Philadelphia: Westminster, 1954.

BENNETT, JOHN C. (ed.). *Nuclear Weapons and the Crisis of Conscience.* New York: Scribner, 1961.

MATTHEWS, Z. K. (ed.). *Responsible Government in a Revolutionary Age.* New York: Association, 1966. A study volume for the 1966 World Conference on Church and Society.

KENNETH JOHNSTONE *et al. Peace is Still the Prize.* London: SCM Press, 1966. A further statement by the group that produced *The Road to Peace* ("Facet Books—Social Ethics Series," No. 10).

Facet Books Already Published

Biblical Series:

Historical Series:

1. *Were Ancient Heresies Disguised Social Movements?*
   by A. H. M. Jones. 1966

2. *Popular Christianity and the Early Theologians*
   by H. J. Carpenter. 1966

3. *Tithing in the Early Church*
   by Lukas Vischer (translated by Robert C. Schultz). 1966

4. *Jerusalem and Rome*
   by Hans von Campenhausen and Henry Chadwick. 1966

Type used in this book
Body, 9 on 11 Janson
Display, Garamond
Paper: White Spring Grove E.F.